A Biblical Basis for World Evangelism

The Great Omission

Robertson McQ

Forewords by Dick L. Van Hal

LITERATURE

P.O. Box 1047
129 Mobilization Drive
Waynesboro, GA 30830 U.S.A.
ph: (706)554-5827

Copyright 1984 by
Robertson McQuilken

First printing, May 1984
Second printing, June 1995
Third printing, April 1999

ISBN: 18845-4323-5

Unless otherwise indicated, the Scripture text used is that of the
New International Version (North American Edition), copyright
1978 by the New York International Bible Society. Used by per-
mission.

Printed in the United States of America

Dedicated to God in honor
of my heroes who have given
their lives to fulfill the
theme of this book—Tom,
Henry, Helen, Lloyd, Virginia,
Lou, Aimee, Anne, Perry,
Marguerite, and Clifford.

Contents

Foreword

Robertson McQuilkin not only is well versed on the trends and strategies of world evangelization, he also has a way with students. When he conducts afternoon seminars on missions at the Urbana student missionary conventions, standing-room-only student crowds invariably pack the hall where he speaks. I know, because more than once I have tried unsuccessfully to get into the room to hear him.

This combination of missiological acumen and missionary "heart" eminently qualifies the president of Columbia Bible College and Columbia Graduate School of Bible and Missions to write this book. This material originally was presented at Reformed Bible College during the winter semester of the 1982–83 academic year. President McQuilkin came to deliver the twelfth annual Baker Mission Lectures, which are made possible by a grant from Grand Rapids publisher Herman Baker. The contents reflect the author's twelve years of missionary service in Japan, his wide acquaintance with evangelical churches in North America, and his awareness of current mission trends throughout the world.

The Great Omission is a penetrating study of Christian missions today, when over half of the world's 4.7 billion people remain unevangelized. Its message is disturbing. McQuilkin indicts the church for its failure to follow the Lord's mandate for evangelization with wholehearted zeal. At the same time, the book brings encouragement to all churches and Christians who will give themselves to learn and to pray, to work and to witness for the completion of the mission task.

This book will profit students, pastors, teachers, and all who are concerned about the Great Commission (Matt. 28:18–20). We are thankful to see McQuilkin's material made available to the public.

Dick L. Van Halsema
President, Reformed Bible College

Foreword

It was June of 1980 when the author met me in a quiet garden at an international evangelism conference in Thailand. That afternoon in the shade of a tree he poured out his heart to me. His burden was the "thrusting out" command of our Lord Jesus Christ: "Ask the Lord of the harvest . . . to send out workers into his harvest field" (Matt. 9:37). We had a profitable season of prayer together in which we shared our mutual burden before the Lord.

The next day he delivered an unforgettable message on the urgent need for laborers. Robertson McQuilkin's heartbeat echoes that of his Savior. In this book he deals with the hindrances that need to be faced by Christians who have made a decision to follow Christ into overseas service, and shares how such problems can be dealt with by prayerful action.

God has a magnificent plan for the salvation of mankind, and it is presented in the Bible. Satan has plans to thwart that which the Savior desires. We are involved in spiritual warfare. I, therefore, highly recommend that people burdened for world missions read this book carefully and see how it might apply to their Christian lives.

John Kyle
Director, Inter-Varsity Missions

Introduction

"**H**ow come?" the voice rang out from the very back of the auditorium. I had just described the world evangelism situation for a group of Urbana students. I had relayed the fact that more than half the world's people not only have never heard the good news of life in Christ; they *cannot* hear because there is no witnessing church among them. At the same time I had briefly outlined the data on the pitifully few who had even attempted to reach those unreached.

" 'How come?' 'How come,' what?" I asked.

The voice from the back of the auditorium rang out again, "With so many unreached people, how come so few are going?"

"That is a very good question," I said. "In fact, I know someone who asks that question every day."

"Who's that?" queried the student at the back of the auditorium.

As I lifted my eyes and gestured heavenward, a hush settled over the audience of several hundred collegians. Indeed, how come? The question has haunted me ever since. I invite you to consider the question.

I believe there are five major answers:

> We don't care that much.
> We don't see very well.
> We think there must be some other way.
> Our prayer is peripheral.
> Someone isn't listening.

1
Three Loves

" 'As the Father has sent me, I am sending you' " (John 20:21).

In that mysterious, overwhelming word of Christ on the night of His resurrection we find people who are moved by three basic motives that cause men to do what they do, to choose what they choose: love for self, love for people, and love for God.

Why one does something is more important than *what* one does or *how* one gets it done. *Why* is more important than one's vocation, activity, knowledge, and skills, because the answer to the question of motive determines the outcome of one's life.

In this brief text we find the disciples, the Father, and the Son all engaged in the same activity—world evangelism. As we shall see, they each had all three of the basic motives. But there is a difference. The controlling motive, the dominant drive was different in each case.

Love for Self

Consider the disciples. Why did they stick it out through three tough years in Jesus' discipleship school? Why did they "hang in there" to the very end? They took the tests and seemed determined to invest their lives in this precarious enterprise. Why?

On one occasion, walking along a dusty Galilean road, the disciples had a heated dispute over who would be greatest (Luke 9:46). When they arrived in Capernaum Jesus asked them what they were quarreling about (Mark 9:34). They were embarrassed and did not want to tell him. So He taught them an object lesson with a humble child, saying, "For he who is least among you all—he is the greatest." (Luke 9:47–48).

On another occasion, the mother of James and John asked top cabinet rank for her sons (Matt. 20:20–21). How did their compatriots feel about this nepotism, a squeeze play on the part of Jesus' cousins to cut them out? Were they humble and spiritual about it? The gospel writer tells us they were angry.

Even at the last solemn gathering of Jesus and His disciples, the Last Supper in the Upper Room, the disciples argued, this time over who should serve (Luke 22:24–27). Apparently there was no servant to wash the dusty feet before reclining for supper, and none of the Twelve was willing to assume that servant role. So a contention developed among them as to who was the most important.

Had the disciples no compassion, no concern for others? They were ready to call down fire on those who were inhospitable to them. They forbade men to preach who had been to the wrong "seminary." They had little time for women, children, and the weak. To be sure, the disciples loved God and His glory, His name, and His kingdom. They certainly loved Jesus. But they were involved in this enterprise, above all else, for what they would get out of it. This is the decisive motive for most people most of the time.

Self-love is not necessarily evil. God Himself appeals to this motive, not only in the unconverted, but in the believer as well. Twice the prophet Ezekiel thunders God's terrifying denunciation against spokesmen for God who do not warn the wicked to flee from their wicked way (Ezek. 3:17–19; 33:7–8). He said, "When . . . you do not speak out to dissuade him from his ways, that wicked man will die for his sin, and I will hold you accountable for his blood" (33:8). Surely this severe Old Testament word is not for the Christian today in his responsibility for wicked men who have not heard of God's judgment and grace? The apostle Paul uses a similar analogy in warning Christians that the outcome of their life's work will be judged and that it *does* make a difference whether one is faithful or unfaithful with what he does with the gospel (I Cor. 3:10–15). Some may be saved, yet through the fire of judgment will lose all hope of reward.

Not only does God warn us of certain loss if we are unfaithful to our responsibilities, He seeks to motivate by assuring us of the great reward that awaits those who are faithful to the missionary mandate:

"Multitudes who sleep in the dust of the earth will awake: some to everlasting life, others to shame and everlasting contempt. Those who are wise will shine like the brightness of the heavens, and those who lead many to righteousness, like the stars for ever and ever" (Dan. 12:2–3).

Love for self—a desire for reward and a fear of loss—are legitimate motives. It is better to obey for a lesser motive than to disobey, but love for self was certainly not the controlling motive of the Father in sending the Son, nor of the Son in coming for our redemption. Love for self is a strong motive, but not strong enough to move a person to great sacrifice and endurance. We go astray when it becomes our controlling motive. Indeed, the dominance of the motive of self-interest among us is enough to explain the poverty of our obedience and the pitiful results of our feeble efforts.

From the fall of Lucifer to the present day, sinful beings have been dominated by love of self. Others must be sacrificed for personal self-fulfillment. Possibly in no other time, however, has this "duty to self" been so zealously undergirded with philosophical justification and promoted and accepted so widely as the only authentic way of life. Daniel Yankelovich, distinguished research professor of psychology at New York University, has documented this major cultural shift in his book, *New Rules: Searching for Self-fulfillment in a World Turned Upside Down*

(New York: Random House, 1981). Yankelovich describes the major social changes in the United States during the 1970s as a move to the determined pursuit of personal self-fulfillment at whatever cost to other values or to other people. One has a duty to himself. Yankelovich documents his thesis that self-denial is on the way out. "The struggle for self-fulfillment is the leading edge of genuine cultural revolution" (p. xx). Speaking of the vast majority of Americans who are committed to this quest, Yankelovich says:

> They speak the tongue of "need" language. They are forever preoccupied with their inner psychological needs. They operate on the premise that emotional cravings are sacred objects and it is a crime against nature to harbor an unfulfilled emotional need (p. 59).

> They embrace a theory of freedom that seems to presuppose that you are free only when you do not commit yourself irrevocably (p. 61).

> Old style success required subordinating the self to external goals, while self-fulfillment seems to require that the self be cultivated, not denied. It is in this conflict between denying the self and nurturing it that we find the key to the normative transformations of our era (p. 85).

> ... The norm is one's duty to one's self, one must follow one's feelings. To break that norm in such a society ... is to do wrong (p. 175).

Yankelovich does not fully approve of this major social shift. For those who determine to live solely

17

on the basis of self-love, pursuing personal fulfillment as their chief goal, he delivers a verdict:

> By concentrating day and night on your feelings,
> potentials, needs, wants and desires, and by learn-
> ing to assert them more freely, you do not become
> a freer, more spontaneous, more creative self; you
> become a narrower, more self-centered, more iso-
> lated one. You do not grow, you shrink (p. 242).

Few Christians would adopt an ethic such as Yankelovich describes, but the virus lives in the atmosphere we breathe. God's purpose of world evangelization will never be fulfilled through people who go
at it primarily to win God's approval or to avoid His
disapproval. Perhaps this malady helps explain why
some churches are so strong in evangelistic outreach
in their own communities while wholly neglecting
the penetration of the unreached people of the world;
and why, on the other hand, some generous missions-
minded churches seldom win those in their own community. If the motivation for a church is to prove
successful in terms of what the "in" group approves,
a great deal of energy can be released in these worthy
activities. But the unworthy motive of self-interest
may be the driving force.

Love for People

"As the Father has sent me, I am sending you"
could simply indicate a similarity of activity. But the
apostle John's commentary on Christ's words clearly
spotlights the motive question (I John 4:7–5:4). The

heart, the attitude, the driving force which moved the Father to send the Son is that which Christ intended to move His disciples in similar obedience. And how was He moved?

> This is how God showed his love among us: He sent his one and only Son into the world that we might live through him. This is love: not that we loved God, but that he loved us and sent his Son as an atoning sacrifice for our sins (I John 4:9–10).

The Father's controlling motive in sending His Son to provide for humankind's salvation was His love for the helpless and hopeless. John tells us that if we have been truly born of God and know God, we will love in the same way (I John 4:7). In fact, "whoever does not love does not know God, because God is love" (v. 8).

God's kind of love is proved by the sacrifice it makes. Our love is proved in the same way (v. 11). Acting from a motive of self-interest is not always wrong, but rather, standing alone it is always inadequate. Self-love will insist on the sacrifice of the other person. When my personal rights, interests, or perceived welfare comes into conflict with the welfare of another, one or the other must be sacrificed. God's kind of love, which is the indispensable mark of membership in God's family, will say no to self-interest in behalf of the other person.

Why is it so difficult to replace a sophisticated way of life with a simple lifestyle in the face of incredible human need in the world? Why is it so difficult to say farewell to warm personal relationships and the security of a loving family and church and commit one's life to penetrating the dark half of the world for the sake of people who are desperately lost? Why will so few abandon an occupation that makes full use of their vocational interests and opportunities to invest life in reaching the multitudes now out of reach of gospel witness? Is it that we don't care? At least it is that we don't care enough. We are committed to choose, act, and live on the basis of self-interest. In the conflict of loves, we choose to save our lives, not lose them. But in saving, we lose.

John not only tells us the nature of love, that it is proved at the point of sacrifice, but he reveals something equally amazing about God's love: He loved us, of all people, when we were not only unworthy, but in fact, were fully worthy of the very opposite, His wrath (v. 9–10). God's kind of love depends not on the lovability of the object, but on the loving character of the one who loves. Perhaps this is why some speak of the need of a lost world as the basic motive for missions. But a world, no matter how lost, will not move me to action while I am mired in self-love. On the other hand, once I am freed to make choices on the basis of compassion for others, the need of lost men and women does indeed become compelling. And what more compelling need is there than billions of people who today face a Christless eternity? This hopeless lostness cannot be photographed as can the need of a starving infant or a motherless child. But the terrifying lostness that envelopes most in this world, pressing them with

inexorable acceleration toward the blackness of hell—
if this does not move us to action, what will?

God's love has no conditions and neither should
ours. Do people have to be nearby for me to love
them? What about half the people of the world who
have no near neighbor to love them in Jesus' name?
Do they have to be "my kind of people"? Must they
be worthy? Must they respond? Must I have a return
on my investment?

Some years ago a student from Columbia Bible
College spent his summer at Hope Town in New York.
(Some would call it "Hopeless Town.") His task was
to diaper a twelve year old and feed a fifteen year
old, to lift, guide, and love those whom society passed
by because they were so unlovable, so physically un-
attractive. There he met a girl with the same heart
and they were married. When Fred and Ronnie returned to school she found a position working with
handicapped children in a government institution,
since she had already completed her training as a
specialist. There she discovered nine-year-old Bonnie, who looked no more than six. She was so abused
she could not talk; her jaw hung open and she was
never able to swallow her saliva. She tried to communicate with grunts. The young couple adopted her
because God's love does not depend on the lovability
of the one being loved, but on the loving character
of the one who loves.

A distraught woman called me on the telephone
and asked if I knew of anyone who could help her
with three teenagers who had just lost their mother
in an automobile accident. Someone needed to keep

them for a few weeks until the relatives could get things together. The children were delinquent and wild, two years behind in school, and lonely. Alcohol and guns were their way of life. Fred and Ronnie moved in with the troubled teenagers, loved them, and won them. Then they led them to faith in Christ, discipled them, and finally adopted them. After graduation they moved back to Hope Town with four adopted children. It was there Ronnie felt life stirring in her own body. With joy they waited the birth of their first born. But then the doctor discovered something else in Ronnie's body—cancer. Next followed the weary round of surgery, radium therapy, pain, and finally remission. They took this as God's green light to head for New Guinea and fulfill their dream of missionary service. There they poured out their lives—and Ronnie's ebbing strength—on primitive ex-cannibals. God's kind of love is for the love-needy, not the love-worthy.

Then, one December just before Christmas, retarded little Bonnie knelt beside her mother's wasted body to pray. In halting, broken words that perhaps only her mother and father—and Jesus—could fully understand, she said, "Dear Jesus, Mommy hurts too much. Please take her to heaven." That night Jesus heard her prayer. Love does not lay conditions. Love gives. And the quality of love is proved by the sacrifice it makes.

How can one become this kind of person? How can one act with the same motivation that the Father had in sending the Son? John explains that God Himself is the source, for God is love (v. 8, 16). We are able to love because God first loved us, and it is by His Spirit in us that the character of the invisible God is created in us. Thus, lost and wandering people can see the reality of a loving God in our lives. In this way, God's love is made complete in us (v. 12). That is, the salvation of a loving God is made visible through people who are infused with His love by being His dwelling place.

Love for others as a controlling motive of life is the way God the Father becomes incarnate in our lives. That was God's motive in sending His Son: He loved us so. But there is one other motive, a motive even higher.

Love for God

God the Father, Son, and Holy Spirit are, by nature, love. From eternity, the ultimate object of their love has been one another. And the Three, bound together in love, surely find this the highest motivation. This love for God is most evident to us in the Son.

What moved the Son to abandon all that He was and had to embrace our sin with its terrible penalty? At the Last Supper He clearly told His disciples: "but the world must learn that I love the Father and that I do exactly what my Father has commanded me" (John 14:31). It was love for the Father that was the all-controlling motive in the Son when He chose to give His life for our redemption. And it will ultimately be that love for God which will enable us to lay down our lives in obedience to the Father for the redemption of a lost world.

To be sure, the Lord Jesus loved people supremely. Four times it is said that the Good Shepherd lays down his life for the sheep (John 10:11, 15, 17, 18). He told us Himself that "greater love has no one than this, that one lay down his life for his friends. You are my friends if you do what I command" (John 15:13–14).

True, for the joy that was set before Jesus, He endured the cross (Heb. 12:2). There was indeed something in it for Himself, something He deemed very precious and longed for. And, of course, another motive was love for "his own" (John 13:1). But ultimately it was love for the Father that dominated in that titanic struggle of the loves: "not my will, but yours be done," Jesus prayed (Luke 22:42). John explains in great detail that such obedience is the proof of love. He wrote, "This is love for God: to obey his commands" (I John 5:2, 3). It will not do to proclaim our love for God and then not obey Him.

Is there any command more forceful than the Great Commission? Is there any greater disobedience than a church squandering its resources on itself for twenty centuries, refusing to live and die in behalf of a world for whom Jesus Christ gave His life?

Love in the Bible is more verb than noun. More than an emotion it is behavior. To love as God loved is to live in behalf of others at any cost to self—indeed, to die in behalf of others if necessary. But we steadfastly refuse to live that way.

Let us go back to the question of the Urbana student at the back of the auditorium: "How come?" Our love life has betrayed us: we don't care that much. Self-love wins too much of the the time. When my rights or my perceived best interests are not compatible with the best interests of another, someone must be sacrificed. Who? That depends on whom I love more. When there is a conflict of interests, does love for self or love for others win out? When the choice is keeping my schedule or healing a brother's hurt, who gets sacrificed? When the choice is another round of junk food or a starving infant in the Sahel, who gets priority? When the choice is keeping a comfortable, successful, secure career or risking life on some lonely frontier, is my will or God's will done?

If I accept the commission to be sent as the Father sent the Son, plans will be laid, not on the basis of how I desire to build my "kingdom," but rather on the basis of how I can best advance the kingdom of God. His purposes in the world and the satisfaction of His heart will control. No longer will personal fulfillment be the motivation for my choices.

But we do not live that way. Why? "How come?" Because we are blinded by preoccupation with self-fulfillment so that we cannot see the world as God sees it; we are deafened by the raucous demands of our personal desires so that we cannot hear His call; we are deadened by persistently choosing for self-interest so that we no longer feel His heartbeat. But Jesus is able to awaken us with those incredible words given first on the night of His mighty resurrection, "As the Father has sent me, I am sending you." Let us respond to His outpouring of love, embracing Him with all our lives until we become even as He is (I John 4:17).

2
Seeing It God's Way

For God so loved the world that he gave his
one and only Son, that whoever believes in him
shall not perish but have eternal life
(John 3:16).

How does one see the world from God's viewpoint? It would be difficult to find a better vantage point than this familiar summary of what the Bible is about. Standing at this overlook we can see what God is like, what God is up to, what God has done, and what God has said. Any one of these should open wide the shutters of our minds to see the world from God's perspective. In combination the vision is clear and sharp—and overwhelming.

What Is God Like?

We begin here because God's purpose, activities, and all that He says flow from what He is.

Certainly God is powerful. The most primitive tribesman, isolated in the jungles of some remote island, cowers before the overwhelming forces of nature and recognizes the power of the unseen. Yet the most educated and influential Christian on his knees also recognizes how helpless and hopeless he would be without the power of an infinite God.

Of course, God is wise. Yet Satan, though no match for God, is powerful and wise beyond our knowing. In the hands of evil, how terrifying and monstrous are authority and power coupled with great intelligence. The difference is that God is more than powerful and wise: He is just and righteous.

When I contemplate my own miserable sinfulness, a powerful, wise, and holy God of justice who gives me what I deserve would be the ultimate terror. Thank God the Evangelist could write the exhilarating, liberating announcement: "God so loved...." The loving character of God makes the salvation of alienated people the primary focus of His attention.

What Is God Up To?

"Man's chief end is to glorify God and to enjoy Him forever," the Westminster Shorter Catechism assures us. As a summary of a human being's proper view of reality, this statement is illuminating and authentic. But how does man fulfill this chief end? Surely by adoring and worshiping his Creator; certainly by obedience, as one is recreated by the Spirit after the moral pattern of God Himself; indeed through the building up of God's church. But the human event that brings greatest glory to God and satisfaction to His heart occurs when a prodigal returns home, when one immigrates out of the kingdom of darkness into the kingdom of His dear Son. Human redemption is the focal point of God's purpose in this world.

Redemption, above all else, is what God is up to. From the Garden of Eden, where He sought the miserable Adam and Eve and promised the triumph of the coming Messiah (Gen. 3:15), down through the ages to the consummation when He welcomes home His bride gathered from every tribe and tongue and people and nation (Rev. 5:9, 10; 19:7), our God, with single-minded determination, is seeking the lost. He is not willing that any should perish. His character and work are spotlighted by glorious fulfillment when ". . . whoever believes in him shall not perish but have eternal life."

What Has God Done?

Folk wisdom has it that actions thunder so loudly about one's character and true intent that feeble words of explanation cannot be heard. What do God's activities demonstrate of His loving character and purpose of world redemption? It is not too much to affirm that every major act of God since creation has been a missionary act.

Even creation does not focus on the intricacies of the atom nor climax with the infinite galaxies. The crescendo builds to a climax in the creation of a being in the likeness of God Himself. This was the overflow of a love which bound the Three in a unity from all eternity. God's desire was to create a being who would

29

have the capacity to fully receive His love and, in turn, to love Him freely and fully. This very likeness to God, the freedom from coerced or programmed choices, set the stage for man's rebellion and alienation.

Man changed but God did not. And thus His purpose shifted from loving companionship with humankind to re-creating the broken pattern of God-likeness so that the loving identity of life could be restored. Thus the sacrificial system, the calling of a special people, the redemption from Egypt, and the giving of the Law all centered in redeeming and restoring.

When God chose to communicate with man in written form, His purpose was the same. The Bible is not a revelation of all of God's activities or purposes from eternity. It is not a record of all human antiquity. It is the story of redemption, climaxing in the greatest event in human history, the Incarnation. This invasion of human life by God Himself was deliberately designed from all eternity, we are told, to provide redemption through the death and resurrection of Jesus Christ. These events, more than anything else Scripture tells us, reveal the purpose and character of God: love reaching out to save hopelessly lost people. What has God done? "God so loved . . . that he gave his one and only Son. . . ." This act of love goes beyond all human comprehension. What could reveal with greater clarity God's character and purpose? What could demonstrate more forceably the center and circumference of His attention?

The next major event, Pentecost, was the descent

of the Holy Spirit to establish the church, to be sure. But the purpose was clear. The entire record of the early church reveals how the apostles viewed the primary purpose of the church toward the world. It was to be God's instrument for world evangelization.

Indeed, it is not too much to say that every major activity of God among men since the Fall has been a saving, missionary act.

What Has God Said?

No matter what the folk wisdom may say, words are not feeble. In fact, words are essential to accurately interpret activity and to fully reveal what is going on in one's mind. God is mysterious and His infinities are far beyond our probing. But He is not a silent God. We can know Him because He has spoken; He has revealed Himself and His will.

We are told that the God of the Old Testament is a narrow-minded, tribal deity. Is this the portrait that Moses draws? Listen to Moses' report of the call of the first selected and segregated person:

> The LORD had said to Abram, "Leave your country, your people and your father's household and go to the land I will show you.
>
> "I will make you into a great nation
> and I will bless you;
> I will make your name great,
> and you will be a blessing.
> I will bless those who bless you,
> and whoever curses you I will curse;

31

and all peoples on earth
will be blessed through you"
(Gen. 12:1–3).

Far from being a narrow-minded tribal deity, from the beginning God was revealed as purposing blessing for the whole world. Did Abraham's descendants lose sight of this? They might have, but God reminded them repeatedly. To Abraham's son Isaac, God renewed the covenant and kept His intentions in focus: ". . . and through your offspring all nations on earth will be blessed . . ." (Gen. 26:4).

Isaac's son, Jacob, might certainly be described as a narrow-minded person of considerable self-interest. But to Jacob also, God clarified His intent: "All peoples on earth will be blessed through you and your offspring" (Gen. 28:14).

The chosen people never forgot that they were chosen. Listen to David in his great celebration of God when the ark was brought to Jerusalem.

> He remembers his covenant forever,
>   the word he commanded, for a
>   thousand generations,
> the covenant he made with Abraham,
>   the oath he swore to Isaac.
> He confirmed it to Jacob as a decree,
>   to Israel as an everlasting covenant:
> "To you I will give the land of Canaan
>   as the portion you will inherit."
>
> When they were but few in number,
>   few indeed, and strangers in it,
> they wandered from nation to nation,
>   from one kingdom to another.

> He allowed no man to oppress them;
>   for their sake he rebuked kings:
> "Do not touch my anointed ones;
>   do my prophets no harm"
>   (I Chron. 16:15–22).

Surely David, like all the chosen people, clearly remembered God's promises to Abraham and the patriarchs. Often, they forgot God's worldwide purpose through them. But not David:

> Give thanks to the LORD, call on his name;
>   make known among the nations what he has
>   done.
>
> Sing to the LORD, all the earth;
>   proclaim his salvation day after day.
> Declare his glory among the nations,
>   his marvelous deeds among all peoples.
>
> Ascribe to the LORD, O families of nations,
>   ascribe to the LORD glory and strength,
>
> Tremble before him, all the earth!
>   The world is firmly established; it cannot be
>   moved.
> Let the heavens rejoice, let the earth be glad;
>   let them say among the nations,
>   "The LORD reigns!"
>   (I Chron. 16:8, 23–24, 28, 30–31).

The psalmist leads us in what must surely be our daily prayer: "May God be gracious to us and bless us" (Ps. 67:1). How hopeless we would be if we received what we justly deserve, so we plead for mercy. We pray, "God bless my work, God bless my health, God bless my family, God bless my church."

33

The psalmist adds, "and make his face shine upon us." If God mercifully forgave us, received us, and graciously prospered us but did not smile on us, assuring us of His favor, what a bleak life we would have. So we rightly ask for God to forgive our sins, bless our affairs, and lovingly companion with us. But why? The psalmist continues: "that thy way be known upon earth, thy saving power among all nations." (RSV) How could the ancient songwriter of Israel declare more clearly his own missionary purpose in total alignment with the purpose of his missionary God?

All this revelation of God's purpose of world redemption was gathered up in the magnificent declarations of the prophet Isaiah:

"Turn to me and be saved,
all you ends of the earth;
for I am God, and there is no other"
(Isa. 45:22).

"It is too small a thing for you to be my servant
to restore the tribes of Jacob
and bring back those of Israel I have kept.
I will also make you a light for the Gentiles,
that you may bring my salvation to the ends of
the earth"
(Isa. 49:6).

I have held Great Commission Workshops with the leadership of many churches, all of which have a strong missions interest. As we examine the biblical basis of missions I have come to expect very little understanding of what the Old Testament has re-

34

vealed concerning a God who loves the world and from the beginning has actively pursued world redemption. Pastors, church leaders, and missions committee members in churches with active missions programs do not know what God has said from the beginning concerning His worldwide intent. I thought that if world missions in the Old Testament is so little understood, perhaps missionary fervor is built on a thorough understanding of New Testament teaching. But in virtually every church, the leadership can recall little world vision in the New Testament prior to the Cross, and has consistently affirmed that the Great Commission was given only on one or two occasions.

Yet Jesus Christ clearly revealed His worldwide intent before Calvary, even when His own primary mission was to "the lost sheep of the house of Israel." At the beginning of His ministry we are told, "God so loved the *world* . . . that *whoever* . . ." (John 3:16; italics mine); and at the end of his ministry He said, "this gospel of the kingdom will be preached *in the whole world* as a testimony. . . ." (Matt. 24:14; italics mine).

Jesus Christ came back to this theme repeatedly on virtually every appearance following His resurrection. He gave this mandate to His church certainly on three occasions, probably on four, and possibly on five occasions recorded in the New Testament.

On the evening following Christ's resurrection He met with the frightened band of disciples and gave them the motive for their mission: "As the Father has sent me, I am sending you" (John 20:21). At His com-

35

mand they went north to Galilee, and there He met them and gave them the model for their mission:

> Then Jesus came to them and said, "All authority in heaven and on earth has been given to me. Therefore go and make disciples of all nations, baptizing them in the name of the Father and of the Son and of the Holy Spirit, and teaching them to obey everything I have commanded you. And surely I will be with you always, to the very end of the age" (Matt. 28:18–20).

The disciples returned then to Jerusalem. I see the events recorded in the last verses of Luke 24 as taking place at this time rather than before they went to Galilee. Here Christ gave His disciples the message of their mission, showing them in the Old Testament how it was prophesied: "and repentance and forgiveness of sins will be preached in his name to all nations, beginning at Jerusalem. You are witnesses of these things" (Luke 24:47, 48).

Our Lord then went with the disciples out toward Bethany to the Mount of Olives. They were still thinking of a political mission of restructuring a very unjust society, and inquired about the timing of Christ's earthly conquest. Our Lord came back to the same theme, giving the method of their mission.

> He said to them: "It is not for you to know the times or dates the Father has set by his own authority. But you will receive power when the Holy Spirit comes on you; and you will be my witnesses in Jerusalem, and in all Judea and Samaria, and to the ends of the earth" (Acts 1:7–8).

We do not know the occasion of the most famous Great Commission recorded in Mark 16:15, but it may well have been yet a fifth occasion following Christ's resurrection in which world evangelization is expressed as the will of God, "Go ye into all the world, and preach the gospel to every creature." (KJV)

If a person is minded to question that this was the clear statement of the will of God, all he need do is examine the interpretation put on these commands by those who were present and heard Him. The disciples who heard these words left us thirty years of action demonstrating how they understood it, and the Holy Spirit considered it important enough to leave a book documenting that interpretation. World evangelization is indeed the expressed will of God.

This, then, is the biblical basis for missions: World evangelization is the *expressed will of God*. Spiritual redemption is the *demonstrated activity of God*.

Evangelism and redemptive activity are expressed as the will of God and the demonstrated activity of God because it is the nature of God so to will and so to act. Love is the *revealed nature of God*. The salvation of lost men is that human event which *brings greatest glory to God*.

Because God is such a God and has given the church such a command, our mandate for action is to make known the good news of life in Christ to every person and to establish a congregation of believers in every place. Until every person has heard with understanding and every community has a witnessing congregation of God's people we may not say to the Father, "It is finished . . . the task which you have given, we have accomplished."

Why is it that we are so far from fulfilling God's design in the world? One reason is that we have not opened ourselves to the full force of the missionary message of Scripture.

"How come?" Because we don't see well. God gives us so clear a revelation of His character, His purpose, His activity, and His will for us, but it seems that we deliberately wear dark glasses with blinders, focusing in Scripture our own small, self-oriented world. Meanwhile the world God loves is lost. May God open our eyes to see the world in focus as He sees it.

3
Lost

*Salvation is found in no one else, for there is
no other name under heaven given to men, by
which we must be saved* (Acts 4:12).

Have you ever experienced the terror of being lost—in some trackless mountain wilderness, perhaps, or in the labyrinth of a great, strange city? Hope of finding your way out fades and fear begins to seep in. You have likely seen that fear of lostness on the tear-streaked face of a child frantically screaming or quietly sobbing because he is separated from his parent in a huge shopping center. Lost. Alone.

Equally terrifying and more common is the feeling of being hopelessly entangled or trapped in a frustrating personal condition or circumstance: alcoholism, cancer, divorce. Incredibly alone! Lost.

The Bible uses the word "lost" to describe an even more terrible condition. Those who are away from the Father's house and haven't found the way back to Him are "lost." Jesus saw the crowds of people surging about Him as sheep without a shepherd, helpless and hopeless, and He was deeply moved.

Worse than being trapped and not knowing the way out is to be lost and not even know it, for then one does not look for salvation, recognize it when it comes, nor accept it when it is offered. That's being lost.

How many are lost in our world? We are told there are 200 million Evangelicals. Some of these are lost no doubt, but at least that many people believe Jesus is the only way of salvation and that through faith in Him one is forgiven and made a member of God's family. Surely some who are not evangelical have saving faith. So let us double the number to a hypothetical 400 million. Those who remain number more than four billion people or nine of every ten on earth. These are the lost—longing for salvation but not finding it, or trusting some other way to find meaning and hope.

The tragedy of this century of exploding population is that three of four people have never heard with understanding the way to life in Christ and, even more tragic, half the people of the world cannot hear because there is no one near enough to tell them. As we approach the end of the second millennium A.D., one of every two on planet earth lives in a tribe or culture or language group that has no evangelizing church at all. If someone does not go in from the outside they have no way of knowing about Jesus.

But are these people in the "dark half of the world" really lost? What of those who have never had a chance, who have never heard—are *any* of them lost? Are *all* of them lost?

Throughout church history there have been those who teach that none will finally be lost. The old universalism taught that all ultimately will be saved because God is good. Not much was heard of this position from the days of Origen in the third century until the nineteenth century when it was revived, especially by the Universalist Church. Simultaneously with the founding of the Universalist Church, which was honest enough to be up front about it and call itself by that name, the teaching began to spread in many mainline denominations.

There are problems with this position. Philosophically, such a teaching undermines belief in the atoning death of Christ. For if all sin will ultimately be overlooked by a gracious deity, Christ never should have died. It was not only unnecessary, it was surely the greatest error in history, if not actually criminal on the part of God for allowing it to happen. Universalism, therefore, philosophically demands a view of the death of Christ as having some purpose other than as an atonement for sin.

Another problem the Universalists faced is that Scripture consistently teaches a division after death between those who are acceptable to God and those who are not. This teaching and that concerning the atonement are so strong in the Bible that Universalists did not accept the authority of Scripture. Thus the marriage between the Universalist Church and the Unitarian Church was quite natural.

A New Universalism arose in the twentieth century which took the Bible more seriously. It was Trinitarian. Christ did die for sinners, and *all* will ultimately be saved on the basis of Christ's provision. Karl Barth and many of his neo-orthodox disciples took such a position. All will be saved because God is all-powerful. His purposes will be accomplished. And He purposes redemption.

There were philosophical and biblical problems with this position also. Philosophically, if all will be saved eventually, for whatever reason, preaching the gospel is not really necessary. Why did Christ make this the primary mission of the church if all will ultimately find acceptance with God with or without the gospel? The more serious problem is biblical: Christ clearly taught of an eternal hell, of a great gulf between the saved and the lost (Luke 16:19–31). In fact, He clearly taught that the majority are on the broad road that leads to destruction (Matt. 7:13–14).

Because Universalism cannot be reconciled with biblical data, there were those who promoted what was called a "Wider Hope." Not all will be saved, but many who have not heard of Christ will be saved because God is just and will not condemn the sincere seeker after truth. The problem is that if sincerity saves in religion, it is the only realm in which it saves. For example, it does not save in engineering. The architect who designed the magnificent John Hancock building in Boston was sincere. The builder was sincere. The glassmaker was sincere. The owner, especially, was sincere. But when the giant sheets of glass began to fall on the streets below, sincerity did not atone for error. Neither does sincerity save in chemistry. We do not say, "If you drink arsenic, sincerely believing it to be Coca-Cola, according to your faith be it unto you." Sincerity does not alter reality. We shall consider the question of God's justice later.

The nineteenth-century doctrine of the Wider Hope

has been superseded by what I have called the "New Wider Hope." According to this teaching those who live by the light they have may be saved on the merits of Christ's death through general revelation. Or, at least, they will be given a chance at death or after death. This is a more conservative version of the New Universalism. Richard Quebedeaux identifies this position as held by some "younger evangelicals," the New Left. A practical problem is that preaching the gospel seems almost criminal, for it brings with it greater condemnation for those who reject it, whereas they conceivably could have been saved through general revelation had they not heard the gospel. In any event, it certainly seems less urgent to proclaim the way of salvation to those who may well be saved without that knowledge. A mutation of this view is the idea that only those who reject the gospel will be lost. This viewpoint is not widespread because it makes bad news of the Good News! If people are lost only if they hear and reject, it is far better not to hear and be saved. On this view it would be better to destroy the message than to proclaim it!

For one committed to the authority of Scripture, our debate concerning the reasonableness of each position must yield to the authority of Scripture. What does Scripture teach concerning the eternal spiritual condition of those who have not heard the gospel?

> "For God so loved the world that he gave his one and only Son, that whoever believes in him shall not perish but have eternal life. For God did not send his Son into the world to condemn the world,

but to save the world through him. Whoever believes in him is not condemned, but whoever does not believe stands condemned already because he has not believed in the name of God's one and only Son."

"Whoever believes in the Son has eternal life, but whoever rejects the Son will not see life, for God's wrath remains on him" (John 3:16–18, 36).

Scripture teaches clearly that there are those who perish and those who do not. Notice that it is those who believe *on Christ*—not simply those who, through their encounter with creation and their own innate moral judgment, believe in a righteous creator—who receive eternal life. God's intent is to "save the world through him [Christ]" (3:17). The word "through" speaks of agency: it is by means of Jesus Christ that a person gains eternal life.

The passage does not deny other agencies, however. The Japanese proverb assures us that many roads lead up famed Mount Fuji but they all reach the top. This is the Japanese way of expressing the viewpoint that all religions will have a good outcome. But Jesus Christ Himself said, "No one comes to the Father except through me" (John 14:6). In other words, Jesus Christ is the *only* agency of salvation.

The New Wider Hope would affirm this. Salvation is by Jesus Christ alone. But, it would hold, that does not mean Jesus Christ must be known by a person for that person to be saved.

Jesus assures us that people will be judged because they have not believed on the *name* (John 3:18). Peter is even more explicit in telling us that there is no salvation in any other *name* given among men (Acts 4:12). Surely it is no accident that the name is so prominent in the Bible, especially in teaching on saving faith. Peter did not say, "in no other person." When a person is named, the identity is settled and ambiguity is done away. Peter does not make room for us to call on the Ground of Being or the great "all." You will be saved, he tells us, if you call on and believe in the name of Jesus of Nazareth, the Messiah.

John, Jesus, and Peter are not the only ones with this emphasis. Paul also speaks to the issue:

> . . . "Everyone who calls on the name of the Lord will be saved." How, then, can they call on the one they have not believed in? And how can they believe in the one of whom they have not heard? And how can they hear without someone preaching to them? And how can they preach unless they are sent? As it is written, "How beautiful are the feet of those who bring good news!" (Rom. 10:13–15).

The ones who call on *the name* are the ones who will be saved. But what of those who have not heard so they cannot call? Paul does not assure us that those who have not heard may simply believe on whatever they have heard. Rather, "faith comes from hearing the message, and the message is heard through the word of Christ" (Rom. 10:17).

Scripture is very clear that there are two kinds of people, both in life and in death: the saved and the lost. It is also very clear on the way of salvation. But still, for those who truly care, questions may remain: Is God loving, powerful, fair, just?

Is God loving? Yes, God is good and that is why men are lost. In love He created a being in His own image, not a robot programmed to respond as the Maker designed. In creating such a being to freely love and be loved, God risked the possibility of such a being rejecting His love in favor of independence or even self-love. Humankind did, in fact, choose this option. Still true to His character, God provided a way back even though the cost was terrible. But the way back must not violate the image of God in man, must not force an obedient response. Rather, the God of love chooses to wait lovingly for the response of love. Those who wish to reject Him may do so.

But is it fair and just for God to condemn those who have not had an opportunity to respond to His offer of grace? The Bible does not teach that God will judge a person for rejecting Christ if he has not heard of Christ. In fact, the Bible teaches clearly that God's judgment is based on a person's response to the truth he has received.

> "That servant who knows his master's will and does not get ready or does not do what his master wants will be beaten with many blows. But the one who does not know and does things deserving punishment will be beaten with few blows. From everyone who has been given much, much will be demanded; and from the one who has been entrusted with much, much more will be asked" (Luke 12:47–48).

> "When you enter a town and are welcomed, eat what is set before you. Heal the sick who are there and tell them, 'The kingdom of God is near you.' But

when you enter a town and are not welcomed, go into its streets and say, 'Even the dust of your town that sticks to our feet we wipe off against you. Yet be sure of this: The kingdom of God is near.' I tell you, it will be more bearable on that day for Sodom than for that town. Woe to you, Korazin! Woe to you, Bethsaida! For if the miracles that were performed in you had been performed in Tyre and Sidon, they would have repented long ago, sitting in sackcloth and ashes. But it will be more bearable for Tyre and Sidon at the judgment than for you. And you, Capernaum, will you be lifted up to the skies? No, you will go down to the depths. He who listens to you listens to me; he who rejects you rejects me; but he who rejects me rejects him who sent me" (Luke 10:8–16).

Judgment is against a person in proportion to his rejection of moral light. All have sinned; no one is innocent. Therefore, all stand condemned. But not all have the same measure of condemnation, for not all have sinned against equal amounts of light. God does not condemn a person who has not heard of Christ for rejecting Him, but rather for rejecting the light he does have.

Not all respond to the light they have by seeking to follow that light. But God's response to those who seek to obey the truth they have is the provision of more truth. To him who responds, more light will be given:

> The disciples came to him and asked, "Why do you speak to the people in parables?"
> He replied, "The knowledge of the secrets of the kingdom of heaven has been given to you, but not

to them. Whoever has will be given more, and he will have an abundance. Whoever does not have, even what he has will be taken from him. This is why I speak to them in parables:

"Though seeing, they do not see;
   though hearing, they do not hear or understand.

   In them is fulfilled the prophecy of Isaiah:

" 'You will be ever hearing but never
   understanding;
   you will be ever seeing but never perceiving.
For this people's heart has become calloused;
   they hardly hear with their ears,
   and they have closed their eyes.
Otherwise they might see with their eyes,
   hear with their ears,
   understand with their hearts
and turn, and I would heal them.'

But blessed are your eyes because they see, and your ears because they hear" (Matt. 13:10–16).

He said to them, "Do you bring in a lamp to put it under a bowl or a bed? Instead, don't you put it on its stand? For whatever is hidden is meant to be disclosed, and whatever is concealed is meant to be brought out into the open. If anyone has ears to hear, let him hear."

"Consider carefully what you hear," he continued. "With the measure you use, it will be measured to you—and even more. Whoever has will be given more; whoever does not have, even what he has will be taken from him" (Mark 4:21–25).

This repeated promise of additional light to those who obey the light they have is a basic and very important biblical truth concerning God's justice and judgment. Cornelius, the Roman officer, responded to the light he had with prayer and good deeds. God did not leave him in ignorance and simply accept him on the basis of his response to the initial light he had received. God sent Peter to him with additional truth (Acts 10). To him who had, more was given. Since this is revealed as God's way of dealing with men, we can be very sure that every person has received adequate light to which he may respond. God's existence and His power are made clearly evident to all people through creation (Rom. 1:18–21) and through each person's innate moral judgment or conscience (Rom. 2:14, 15). To the one who responds obediently, God will send additional light.

Of course, His method for sending this light is a human messenger. Paul makes clear in his letter to the church at Rome (10:14, 15) that the solution to the terrible lost condition of men is the preacher who is sent, the "beautiful feet" of he who goes. Ultimately, then, the problem is not with God's righteousness, but with ours.

But suppose no one goes? Will God send some angel or some other special revelation? On this, Scripture is silent and, I believe, for good reason. Even if God did have such an alternative plan, were He to reveal that to us, we who have proved so irresponsible and disobedient would no doubt cease altogether obedience to the Great Commission.

But the question will not go away. How does one respond in a Japanese village when a new convert inquires, "What about my ancestors?" My response is simple: I am not the judge. "Will not the Judge of all the earth do right?" (Gen. 18:25). Abraham was pleading with God for the salvation of innocent people who did not deserve to be condemned and destroyed along with the guilty. He was appealing to God's justice, and God responded with grace more than Abraham dared ask. This crucial question recorded in the first book of the Bible is answered in the last: "Yes, Lord God Almighty, true and just are your judgments" (Rev. 16:7). We are not called as judge—either of God whose ways we do not fully know nor of man whose destiny we are not called upon to settle. Rather, we are commissioned as His representatives to find the lost, declare amnesty to the captive, release the prisoner.

We may not be able to prove from Scripture with absolute certainty that no soul since Pentecost has ever been saved by extraordinary means without the knowledge of Christ. But neither can we prove from Scripture that a single soul has been so saved. If there is an alternative, God has not told us of it. If God in His revelation felt it mandatory not to proffer such a hope, how much more should we refrain from such theorizing. It may or may not be morally right for me to think there may be another way and to hope there is some other escape. But for me to propose it to other believers, to discuss it as a possibility, is certainly dangerous, if not immoral. It is almost as wrong as writing out such a hope so that those who are under the judgment of God may read it, take hope, and die. So long as the truth revealed to us identifies only one way of escape, this is what we must live by and proclaim.

Consider the analogy of a security guard charged with the safety of residents on the tenth floor of a nursing home. He knows the floor plan posted in a prominent place, and it is his responsibility in case of fire to get the residents to the fire escape which has been clearly marked. Should a fire break out and lives be put in jeopardy, it would be his responsibility to get those people to the fire escape. If he discusses with the patients or with a colleague the possibility of some other unmarked fire escape or recalls to them the news report he read of someone who had jumped from the tenth floor of a building and survived, he could surely be charged with criminal negligence. He must live and labor in obedience to the facts that are certain and not delay to act. He must not lead people astray on the basis of conjecture or logical deduction from limited information.

When all has been said that can be said on this issue, the greatest remaining mystery is not the character of God nor the destiny of lost people. The greatest mystery is why those who are charged with rescuing the lost have spent two thousand years doing other things, good things, perhaps, but have failed to send and be sent until all have heard the liberating word of life in Christ Jesus. The lost condition of human beings breaks the Father's heart. What does it do to ours?

In a dream I found myself on an island—Sheep Island. Across the island sheep were scattered and lost. Soon I learned that a forest fire was sweeping across from the opposite side. It seemed that all were doomed to destruction unless there were some way of escape. Although there were many unofficial maps, I had a copy of the official map and there discovered that indeed there is a bridge to the mainland, a narrow bridge, built, it was said, at incredible cost.

My job, I was told, would be to get the sheep across that bridge. I discovered many shepherds herding the sheep who were found and seeking to corral those who were within easy access to the bridge. But most of the sheep were far off and the shepherds seeking them few. The sheep near the fire knew they were in trouble and were frightened; those at a distance were peacefully grazing, enjoying life.

I noticed two shepherds near the bridge whispering to one another and laughing. I moved near them to hear the cause of joy in such a dismal setting. "Perhaps the chasm is narrow somewhere, and at least the strong sheep have opportunity to save themselves," said one. "Maybe the current is gentle and the stream shallow. Then the courageous, at least, can make it across." The other responded, "That may well be. In fact, wouldn't it be great if this proves to be no island at all? Perhaps it is just a peninsula and great multitudes of sheep are already safe. Surely the owner would have provided some alternative route." And so they relaxed and went about other business.

In my mind I began to ponder their theories: Why would the owner have gone to such great expense to build a bridge, especially since it is a narrow bridge and many of the sheep refuse to cross it even when they find it? In fact, if there is a better way by which many will be saved more easily, building the bridge is a terrible blunder. And if this isn't an island, after all, what is to keep the fire from sweeping right across into the mainland and destroying everything? As I pondered these things I heard a quiet voice behind me saying, "There is a better reason than the logic of it, my friend. Logic alone could lead you either way. Look at your map."

There on the map, by the bridge, I saw a quotation from the first undershepherd, Peter: "For neither is there salvation in any other, for there is no other way from the island to the mainland whereby a sheep may be saved." And then I discerned, carved on the old rugged bridge itself, "I am the bridge. No sheep escapes to safety but by me."

In a world in which nine of every ten people is lost, three of four have never heard the way out, and one of every two cannot hear, the church sleeps on. "How come?" Could it be we think there must be some other way? Or perhaps we don't really care that much.

4
Power Failure

"But you will receive power when the Holy Spirit comes on you; and you will be my witnesses in Jerusalem, and in all Judea and Samaria, and to the ends of the earth" (Acts 1:8).

These words form the table of contents for the short book that follows. Instead of the traditional title for the book, "The Acts of the Apostles," some Bible scholars have suggested the title, "The Acts of the Holy Spirit." For our consideration I would suggest as a title for this drama the other side of the same theme: "The Devil's Frustration, Acts II and III."

Just fifty days before Act II opens, Act I was completed. At the climax of the cosmic struggle of the ages, there is a great celebration in hell. Satan thinks he has won the war, for the King of Kings has been destroyed. Ever since the birth of Jesus of Nazareth, Satan had made attempts on His life. This time he has succeeded. Satan and his scholars are students of Scripture and, no doubt, students of prophecy. Perhaps that is one reason prophecy is not always specific. Apparently, not finding the resurrection of the Messiah predicted in the Old Testament, he had overlooked the great strain of teaching that the Messiah would live forever. How hell must have reeled under the impact of the news of that first Easter Lord's Day morning: Jesus Christ is risen, triumphant, and all authority in heaven and on earth has been given to Him.

Perhaps Satan was still in a state of shock when the curtain lifted for Act II of the drama: the Holy Spirit descended, and the church was born. On the other hand, he may not have considered it a particularly significant event, for his long experience with humankind would not condition him to be deeply concerned about any organization of human beings, no matter how many promises of commitment they might make to his enemy, the Lord God. This was his second fatal error. Apparently he did not take seriously another prediction: "I will build my church, and the gates of Hades will not overcome it" (Matt. 16:18).

The Book of Acts reports the birth of the church and the early days of the fulfillment of Christ's prophecy. "Gates" symbolized authority and power. He might have said the "Pentagon" of the kingdom of darkness shall not overcome the church. Others interpret the prophecy to indicate that Satan and his kingdom will not even be able to resist the power of the church, that the church will surely overcome (a startling, incredible prediction!).

Follow the record for a few short months in the

early days of this church. Soon after Pentecost there was the healing of a well-known beggar-cripple (chap. 3). What would the Enemy do? Give up? The counterattack is recorded in chapter 4 where the religious leaders apparently reported to the civil authorities the preaching of the resurrection and the response of the people. The top police officer, second in command to the high priest, came and arrested the two leaders, Peter and John. That is the way to stop a movement: immobilize the leadership. Peter and John were rebuked and warned. How did they respond? "Judge for yourselves whether it is right in God's sight to obey you rather than God. For we cannot help speaking about what we have seen and heard" (Acts 4:19–20). And the result? "Many of them who heard the message believed, and the number of men grew to about five thousand" (Acts 4:4).

The first attack had failed. The next attack was not from the outside, but through internal corruption. It was the devil, we are told, who put it into the hearts of Ananias and Sapphira to put on a religious act to impress people with their godliness (chap. 5). The response of the church was swift and the response of the Holy Spirit, jealous for the purity and power of the fledgling church, was severe. What would have happened to a church without discipline? But the early church, purified, surged forward with strength: "more and more men and women believed in the Lord and were added to their number" (5:14).

The second attack had failed, so the Enemy launched an even heavier blow against the leadership. This time the political authorities took the initiative and arrested the entire leadership of the church. God intervened supernaturally and the apostles were released (5:19). Watch carefully the response of these leaders who had all fled on the night of the crucifixion. In the morning they returned to the center of the warfare, the Temple itself, and began once again to proclaim Jesus Christ as Lord! How embarrassed were the authorities who had convened the supreme court only to discover they had no prisoners! This time the apostles were flogged to punctuate the warning, but their response was the same: Peter and the other apostles answered and said, "we must obey God rather than men!" (5:29). In fact, "The apostles left the Sanhedrin, rejoicing because they had been counted worthy of suffering disgrace for the Name. Day after day, in the temple courts and from house to house they never stopped teaching and proclaiming the good news that Jesus is the Christ" (5:41, 42). What was the result? "In those days . . . the number of the disciples was increasing. . . ." (6:1).

Satan's third attack had failed. The next assault was again internal. There was an organizational breakdown, perhaps because of the rapid growth. On the other hand, maybe it was neglect on the part of the leadership. The minority group was receiving unfair treatment. As is so often the case, the newcomers were discriminated against. What was the response of the church? Typically, there were hurt feelings and envy. This led to complaining, and complaining led to division. What was the response of the leaders? In this instance it was practical wisdom and fairness. Since they had failed in their supervising responsibility, they decided to appoint additional leaders who would have time to adequately administer the affairs of the church and insure fair treatment for all.

The response of the *people* was generosity. In choosing those who would supervise the distribution of food to the poor, the church did a remarkable thing. It choose all seven from the minority party! And the result? "So the Word of God spread. The number of disciples in Jerusalem increased rapidly, and a large number of priests became obedient to the faith" (6:7). Perhaps it was this remarkable response of the church to a very natural division in their midst that won those priests, some of whom no doubt had been at the forefront of opposition to Jesus Christ and the early church.

Satan's fourth attack failed, so the next was an all-out attack. One of the most effective men in this emerging group of new leadership, Stephen, was arrested, rebuked, flogged, and executed. With that, a great persecution of the entire church erupted so that the people were scattered everywhere. What was their response to this attack of the Enemy? Did they go underground? "They were all scattered throughout Judea and Samaria. . . . Those who had been scattered went about preaching the word" (8:1–4). (RSV)

"I will build my church," Christ had promised, "and the gates of Hades will not overcome it." (Matt. 16:18). Notice that the church's victory was the direct result of the church's response to the Enemy's attack. What kind of church is a frustration to the Enemy?

What kind of church fulfills the prophecy of Jesus Christ?

These were God's unstoppables. Following Pentecost they shook Jerusalem to its foundation. Persecution initially followed and they spread to surrounding Judea. Samaria was next, followed by explosive witness to neighboring provinces.

Act III of this incredible drama follows with the story of Paul, the converted persecutor, who extended the kingdom of God to some of the "uttermost parts of the earth."

Notice a brief description of the kind of church that fulfills God's purposes and overcomes the Enemy:

> They were all filled with the Holy Spirit and spoke the word of God boldly.
> All the believers were one in heart and mind. No one claimed that any of his possessions was his own, but they shared everything they had. With great power the apostles continued to testify to the resurrection of the Lord Jesus, and much grace was with them all. There were no needy persons among them. For from time to time those who owned lands or houses sold them, brought the money from the sales and put it at the apostles' feet, and it was distributed to anyone as he had need (Acts 4:31b–35).

As we watched the drama of the early church unfold, we saw a church with incredible courage. We saw leaders, gifted of God to evangelize, but we also saw the witness of the whole group—they all spoke the Word of God with boldness. This powerful and united witness was grounded firmly in a fellowship of unconditional, mutual commitment and interdependence. The unity of God's people was seen in purifying discipline, in common-sense decision, and in generous response to division in the church. But in this passage the unity is seen as a commitment to guarantee the welfare of other "family" members at whatever personal cost. This guarantee reached out to the spiritual condition and the material as well.

It is not just any church that can withstand the attacks of the Enemy and press the battle victoriously to the uttermost parts of the earth. It is the church of total self-giving and bold witness. A church that is divided, selfish, and impotent in witness should never presume to claim the promise Jesus Christ made to His church. Such a church is nothing more than a pitiful parody of God's intent, a usurper, planting the glorious banner of the church amid the rubble and ruins of a fortress long since laid waste by the Enemy.

What hope is there? How can a weak and divided, self-centered church become a true church and claim the promises of the Lord of the church, partaking of His authority and accomplishing His purposes? Note the response of the early church once again: "On their release, Peter and John went back to their own people and reported all that the chief priests and elders had said to them. When they heard this, they raised their voices together in prayer to God" (Acts 4:23–24a).

Why did they not appoint a committee to draft a resolution? Why did they not open the floor for debate, hammer out a compromise solution, and send a delegation to negotiate with the authorities? The

61

secret of victory in the church of Jesus Christ lies precisely in that first response to a frontal attack by the Enemy: "they raised their voices in prayer to God."

A praying church is a victorious church. A prayerless church is a defeated church, defeated even before the battle begins. These raw recruits in God's army knew their source of strength. Every time there was testing or opportunity they gathered in prayer. In fact, they were together daily in prayer (2:42, 46). And their leaders apparently spent most of their time praying when they were not teaching and preaching (6:4). Acts 4 gives a sample of what they actually prayed.

The early church began their prayer by acclaiming the glory of the God who made heaven and earth, the sea, and all that is in them (4:24). Thus they began with focusing on God's greatness and power. That strengthens faith! Then they moved immediately to pray according to the revealed will of God (4:25). They quoted God's promises and claimed them in that hour of testing. They established a Bible-based authority to pray according to the will of God. In doing this, they identified with God's purposes in the world. God purposed to provide redemption through the sacrifice of the Messiah (4:26, 27, 28). How could God turn them down when they came on such a basis?

Finally they made their request. What request would I have made under those circumstances? Certainly for deliverance. Possibly I would suggest to the Lord various ways in which He might change the circumstances to make life more comfortable or success easier. But these early saints cried out to God simply for boldness that they might speak the Word with power (4:29). They also asked that God would be with them in revealing His mighty power (4:31).

Why are we so weak and impotent? Why have we watched in our lifetime as the number of lost people has increased geometrically? Are we not weak in impact for God because we are weak in time spent with God?

God acts in response to the united prayer of faith of an obedient people: "After they prayed, the place where they were meeting was shaken. And they were all filled with the Holy Spirit and spoke the word of God boldly" (4:31).

Thus it has been and thus it will ever be. The Holy Spirit rolls back the powers of darkness not through an invasion and conquest of those powers, but through an invasion and conquest of His own people. Those who company with God, who are experienced in the spiritual warfare of intercession, are the people who know the power of God to live a supernatural quality of life and to minister in miracle power.

We should not be surprised that God's plan is thus. When Jesus saw the crowds of lost people and was deeply moved, He did not command the disciples to go and rescue the lost. Not then. First, He commanded them to "Ask the Lord of the harvest, therefore, to send out workers into his harvest field" (Matt. 9:38). I have become convinced that the church will never complete God's purposes of redemption in the world in obedience to His great command unless God the Holy Spirit powerfully thrusts laborers into the harvest field. And we are commanded to participate in this sending out of workers first of all through prayer.

And what are we doing? A recent study indicated that American Evangelicals spend about four minutes a day in prayer and their pastors seven (*Church Around the World*, Vol. 2, 1981). Our corporate prayer for world evangelization is even more pitiful. After holding Great Commission Workshops in many strongly missions-minded churches across the nation, I am convinced that those churches which are strongest in sending and supporting missionaries average no more than two or three minutes a week in united prayer for the missionary enterprise. Is there any wonder that the church has experienced a massive power failure so that darkness envelopes the world for which we are to be lights? The connection with our source of power is so tenuous, so sporadic, that we flicker and often seem simply to blink out.

Is there no hope?

God intervened in the life of the early church when they were not immediately obedient to His command to reach out into the neighboring areas and to the distant unreached of the world. He scattered them through persecution. But God scattered a Spirit-anointed, praying people. I am not confident that the result would be the same today if the church in North America were so scattered. The incredible spiritual harvest in Korea and now in China is surely a result of a strong church's response to terrible persecution.

American churchmen, visiting Korea, are greatly

impressed with the incredibly rapid growth of the church. To see a local congregation with more than two hundred thousand members or to witness a world evangelism congress with more than two million in attendance is a moving experience. Many of these American churchmen have rightly pinpointed the source of such overwhelming spiritual power— prayer. Before one such evangelism congress where hundreds of thousands of parents offered their children for missionary service and tens of thousands of young people offered their lives for such service, more than half a million people spent the night on their knees—on the concrete, in the rain.

Korean churches whose people live in crowded conditions purchase mountains filled with caves for the purpose of private prayer. To these mountains thousands of Christians go for days of fasting and prayer.

We learn of the Korean's success and return to our homeland and seek to hold a prayer rally or to establish a prayer retreat center. But such a spirit of prayer does not come through organization, nor can it be induced instantly through well-planned programs. The church of Korea was born in revival and has been carried along by the prayers of its suffering people through decades of deadly persecution, bitter warfare, and depression. For more than thirty years, long before the great expansion and giant churches, the people of God have gathered each morning of the week for united intercession.

Perhaps a nonpraying church can become a praying church without God's discipline, but there is another invasion of God that is absolutely essential. When the apostles, after three years of intimate companionship with Jesus, still went astray in eschatological inquiry and continued devotion to wrong-headed, earth-bound goals, Christ said to them, "Do not leave Jerusalem, but wait for the gift my Father promised, which you have heard me speak about . . . . in a few days you will be baptized with the Holy Spirit" (Acts 1:4–5). So they waited in prayer until the Holy Spirit came upon them in power.

The need of the church today is for revival quickening that will give it rebirth as a praying people who become, once again, a mighty force for God. Note that the early Christians and their leaders did not go about business-as-usual and wait for God to take the initiative. They gathered together in united, believing prayer until God poured out His Holy Spirit. Can there be any question but that the blindness and impotence of the church today—the power failure— is because we are not a praying people?

I see great hope, however. The student movements that are springing up across the nation are borne along by prayer. There is a commitment to united prayer warfare that I have not witnessed in recent generations. It is common for students on dormitory floors or in regional or national gatherings to set aside their schedules and spend the night in prayer. In the conventions they call to plan strategy for world evangelization, prayer is the predominant item on the agenda. It would seem that God is bypassing the older generation to raise a people with clear vision of the task remaining, of total commitment to see it done, and determination to accomplish it in God's way, through united, believing prayer by an obedient people.

With the need so incredibly great, why is the church so impotent? "How come?" In the first place, we don't see very well from God's perspective. Furthermore, we are self-oriented and don't care that much about the lostness of people. But above all, we are powerless because our prayer is peripheral, a tepid formality, while God is calling us to mighty intercessory warfare.

5
Who's Calling?

"Whom shall I send? And who will go for us?"
Isa. 6:8)

*"I looked for a man among them who would
build up the wall and stand before me in the
gap on behalf of the land so I would not have
to destroy it, but I found none"* (Ezek. 22:30).

Redemption is indeed God's chief
purpose toward this world. His nature demands it.
God loved the world so much that He gave the ultimate gift. Unlike His church, He was not willing that
any should perish. Greg Livingston, of the North Africa Mission, tells of his conversation with a strong
Christian elder in Lebanon. Livingston asked, "Don't
you care that these Arab Muslims are going to hell?"
The elder responded, "Well, brother, between you
and me, that's probably the best place for them."

When the shock of such a response passes, we know
in the depths of our spirit that this is precisely the
way the church of Jesus Christ in each generation
has behaved, no matter what the rhetoric.

Not only does God's character put world evangelism central in His purpose, man's lost condition de-

69

mands it. The population explosion is so great that more people will be born in the last quarter of this century than in the whole history of mankind prior to 1973 (cf. John V. Taylor, *Enough is Enough* [London: SCM Press, 1975], p. 14). This is the scope of the lostness of humanity. Is there no hope? Does not the need so far exceed our resources as to confront us with an impossible mission? No, for God has a viable plan, and He has assured us in advance that it will succeed. The only question is: in which generation?

God has designated and stands ready to equip those who will be sent by the church to win to faith people who have not heard, and to establish congregations where they do not exist. These apostles are the only plan God has. Furthermore, they are the only plan He needs. But no generation in nearly two thousand years of church history has produced the task force necessary to reach the world. Is this because God has not called adequate numbers? Or is it because someone is not listening?

The evangelical churches of the United States now have about thirty-seven thousand career foreign missionaries. About nine thousand of these are engaged in full-time evangelism, some in church-starting evangelism. How many would be needed to penetrate the dark half of the world, plant a gospel witness among every people and share the glorious liberating word of redemption with all mankind? Estimates range from five to ten times that number.

But the picture is even darker than it seems. The number of cross-cultural representatives of the church has virtually plateaued during the last two decades.

70

Even the bright hope of the new movement of third world missionaries has not changed the totals greatly. Besides this, since the flood of new missionaries following World War II is reaching retirement age, decline seems inevitable.

Perhaps we do not have a sufficient support base to put an adequate force into the field. Before the days of William Carey, the father of the modern Protestant missionary movement, the Moravians from Herrnhut considered a support base of four adequate to keep one missionary at the front. In such an atmosphere of spiritual vitality, we would need less than one million Evangelicals, and the small state of South Carolina could take care of evangelizing the world. But perhaps this is unrealistic. In World War II it was said that fifteen personnel were needed to keep one man at the front. If this proved true in spiritual warfare, three million support "troops" should be adequate and the Evangelicals of California could finish the task.

In point of fact, we are told there are not three but *forty* million Evangelicals in the United States. We know that this support base is fully adequate, even at present levels of providing workers and finance. At least a million have responded to the call to some form of full-time Christian ministry. If only ten or twenty percent of these already involved in Christian ministry were dispatched by the churches, the task could be accomplished. But the truth is, less than one percent of full-time Christian workers are engaged in evangelistic ministry among the unevangelized of the world. Is this the way the Commander-in-Chief would assign His troops? Or is someone not listening?

Static

Perhaps more would hear God's call if there were not so much static. Well-meaning advocates of world missions get hold of a truth, strip it of complementary truths, and use it to pry loose some of God's frozen people. The intent is good, but the results are bad. Truth made to stand alone rarely stands long and never stands straight, as A. W. Tozer has assured us. Partial truth is often a distortion and this can only cause confusion and create static for those who would tune in to God's signal. Consider the plight of the earnest believer seeking God's will for his life when he hears the following:

Everyone should head toward missionary service until God stops him.
No one should become a missionary if he can be happy doing anything else.
If you haven't had a call, you must not be listening because Christ gave the call two thousand years ago. You are already called!
The Great Commission is all the call you need.
Don't move until God gives you a call.
The need constitutes the call.
No one has a right to hear the gospel twice until every one has heard it once.
Grow where you were planted.

Each of these common exhortations is intended to highlight an aspect of God's truth concerning the call to missionary service. Yet by highlighting only part of the truth, well-meaning advocates often produce confusion, frustration, and disillusionment with The Cause. How then, does one tune out the static and tune in to God's clear call?

Tuning in

There is only one place to begin. One who does not acknowledge the absolute lordship of Christ in every choice of life cannot hear any call from God. In fact, for him there may not be any other call from God. If Jesus Christ alone is absolute Lord of my life, He alone has the right to make the greatest of all choices for me: how will I invest my life? Until such an unconditional commitment to the will of God has been made, a person who "tries to do God's will" is only deceiving himself (or perhaps only trying to deceive his audience).

But once the question is settled as to who is in control, cannot the disciple hold God responsible to get him where he ought to be? Some say so, and thus do not hold up to God's people the teaching of Scripture concerning world evangelization nor the present condition of the world and the church. But this is a misunderstanding of what it means to acknowledge Jesus Christ as Lord. Obedience to God is never fulfilled through mere passive availability. It demands active involvement. "Eagerly desire the greater gifts," says the apostle Paul (I Cor. 12:31). It is no accident

73

that he put at the top of his list (v.28) the apostolic ability, the calling to evangelize where Christ is not known and start the church where there is none. "Go for it," Paul would say in the contemporary idiom, "and keep on going for it with active involvement."

But our pews are filled with n on-combatants, our pulpits with slot-fillers, waiting for a jolt from heaven. George Murray, of the Evangelical Alliance Mission, tells us that for years he was "willing to stay, but planning to stay." Not until he became "willing to stay, but planning to go" did God move him to Italy.

Perhaps this inertia of a passive "obedience" is the reason for the outcome of past Urbana conventions where thousands of young people stood to acknowledge Christ as Lord and to pledge to do God's will. Says missionary researcher Ed Dayton, "If history repeats itself ten thousand young people will state their willingness to be used by God in the most magnificent calling in the world. If history repeats itself perhaps less than five hundred will ever make it" (New World Missions" World Vision, 1979).

Acknowledging Christ as Lord must be more than a transient stirring of emotions or a passive acknowledgemnt that we are not the owners and operators of our lives. It demands an active pursuit of God's purposes in the world. It means commitment of one's total life to make the greatest possible impact for Jesus Christ on this generation. And for those who are not yet certain of God's vocational appointment in life, true discipleship must surely include complete openness to this most needed and most neglected of all vocations: pioneer missionary evangelism.

Note that active involvement is not some high level of spiritual achievement. This unconditional "yes" to God is the basic definition of what discipleship is.

Once one has made the initial unconditional commitment to active pursuit of the will of God, how does he make certain of his personal role? The decision to make Christ Lord has tuned him in to God's signal. Now, how does he keep climbing on course?

Climbing on Course

Even though the initial decision has been made to obey every signal from the Commander-in-Chief, the signal can be distorted through interference. God often sends His signals through fellow combatants, and thus we may get mixed signals.

For example, we hear that "every person is either a mission field or a missionary." By calling every true Christian a missionary, the idea is to involve every believer in sharing his faith as a way of life. The intent is good, but confusion reigns because the earnest seeker for God's will is lead to believe that there are no distinctions among Christians, that every Christian vocation, if not every vocation, is of equal value. In this view of the cause of world evangelism, role distinction is blurred and all roles appear of equal significance.

The underlying truth of this notion is that the most important role for any individual is that for which God has equipped him through natural and Spirit-

75

given ability. The most important thing for the congregation is that each Christian function in the capacity for which God has equipped him. The church in which ten or twenty percent of the members seek to fulfill all the functions of the body is crippled, if not paralyzed. And how distorted and ineffective is the church in which members seek to function in roles to which God did not call them! But the fact that all members are needed does not mean that all roles are of equal importance for God's cause.

Perhaps we have been beguiled into accepting this viewpoint through a popular, if misguided, notion that all secular occupations are of equal value. I received from the headquarters of a major corporation suggestions for a church bulletin insert on "The Dignity of Work Day."

> We have failed to recognize that the carpenter [and] the cosmetologist are *just* as valuable, *just* as worthy, and *just* as much needed as the doctor. . . .

Most people would not have to reflect much on the relative disadvantages of living in a town where there were no doctor or where they were deprived of the presence of a cosmetologist. No one, of course, would want his physician to decorate his wife's face any more than he would want the local cosmetologist to remove his ruptured appendix. But to hold that all vocations are of equal value to society is absurd.

The same goes for the church. The Corinthian error was placing an inordinate value on the wrong gift. Rather than seeking the gift of speaking in tongues, the Corinthians were enjoined to pursue the virtue of love and the gifts of higher value to God's cause, especially apostolic evangelism, prophetic preaching, and Spirit-filled teaching (I Cor. 12:28).

> To say that a believer can serve God in any vocation is one thing; to go on to say that it does not matter what vocation he chooses is something else . . . . It is foolish to say that one can advance the cause of Christ as much in one vocation as in another. . . . True, one can serve God in any capacity, and in his sovereign plan everyone has a niche to fill. But we cannot go on to assert that all careers are equally crucial in the advancement of God's kingdom. (David Kucharsky, "Careers with Christian Impact," *Christianity Today* [September 24, 1971], p. 14.)

No, not everyone is a missionary and not all roles are of equal value in fulfilling God's purpose of world evangelization.

The crucial role in God's plan of redemption is the evangelistic church starter. To be sure, he must be supported by a complement of support personnel. Perhaps that is one reason 75 percent of all missionaries sent from the United States are actually serving the church elsewhere, rather than serving full-time in evangelism or church starting. Thus, among missionaries, there are many vocations.

By lumping together various vocations under the term "missionary" we may add another element of confusion for a person seeking to know God's will for life investment. By "missionary" we have gradually come to mean someone who serves in a culture or country other than his own and is paid for that service, whatever it may be, by Christian people in his sending church. Thus, "the missionary call" has become a call to a location, rather than to a vocation. One may be teaching theological education, pastoring a church, nursing the ill, digging wells, or doing itinerant evangelism. He is a missionary, in our contemporary understanding, so long as he is doing it full-time and is paid for that activity by Christians in the homeland. This change of focus from an apostolic evangelistic vocation to the entire enterprise of doing good away from home need not prove fatal. Actually, these are all ministries which the church ought to provide. And if the recruit sorting out his "calling," the missions assigning tasks, and the church leaders in the receiving church can get together on what the specific vocational call is, God's cause will be advanced.

But this change of definition and focus of attention from pioneering to interchurch service will prove fatal to countless millions of people if the lack of pioneer missionary evangelists goes unnoticed because of other good missionary activity. We must recapture the New Testament vision and thrust for world evangelization through those who are called and commissioned for the task of extending God's kingdom.

But how does one get a "call" of any kind? Here again there are mixed signals from God's people. Some hold that one should not go into any Christian vocation without a Pauline-type of special word from God. Did not Christ specifically call the Twelve to a particular role? Were not the prophets of the Old Testament chosen before birth and set apart by God to a holy vocation? On the other hand, there are those who assure us that the missionary call is no more special than the call to any other vocation, Christian or secular. It is a matter of guidance. Just as the brick mason must be very certain that this role is God's will for his life, so the missionary should be certain of his vocation.

After years of involvement in the enterprise of selecting, training, sending, and deploying the missionary task force, I am convinced that there is an element of truth in both positions. Certainly there was in both the Old Testament and the New Testament a kind of work that was set apart from ordinary vocations, a holy office, role, or vocation. In the New Testament church a person was identified by the specific ability or enabling that God gave him, but he was also set aside through the concurrence of God's people. There was an inner conviction and compulsion, and there was also the external validation by the church. Thus through evidence of ability, an inner conviction, and the endorsement of the church, the call is supernatural and special, different from ordinary guidance.

On the other hand, even for a person with so spectacular a call as Paul on the road to Damascus, we find the very strong element of ordinary Christian guidance. Paul did not go on the first call! As a matter of fact, he returned home to Tarsus. It was there a friend found him and issued a very ordinary, human call to join the leadership team in Antioch (Acts 11:26). Here again, Paul apparently settled down as one of the pastors of the church in Antioch until God, this time through the church as a whole, thrust him out into his first missionary activity. You might even say it was on the third call that Paul found his vocation. Yet God is the one who superintended the circumstances of his life through ordinary Christian guidance. In Acts 16 we read of Paul's attempt to penetrate Ephesus ahead of God's timing. He was deflected from this by God Himself. He then made a second attempt at God's will, traveling north toward Bithynia until once again he was stopped. This time the team headed west, the only direction remaining, where God positioned him at Troas for the great leap over into Europe. Although Paul had been "called" and set apart for the apostolic evangelistic vocation years before, it was through a process of step-by-step guidance that God led him into actual missionary activity and along the path of evangelistic advance.

How do these two concepts of "call" and "guidance" come together? Some may begin, like Paul, with a special intervention in life that settles the question of vocational call once for all. Such a person will then embark on a lifetime of seeking to follow God's guiding directions to accomplish that great vision or goal which God has given. On the other hand, others may find themselves following the principles of Scripture and obeying the impulses of the Spirit and the counsel of the elders, taking into account the circumstances of life, until there comes a time when the conviction is settled that God has designated them for some particular ministry. That conviction is just as certainly a call to holy vocation or a life set apart for a special ministry, as though the person had begun with a heavenly vision.

How then does one determine whether or not God has in mind some form of missionary vocation? The inner response of a person's spirit to the revelation of God's program in the world and its present state should catapult every true disciple into total involvement in that enterprise. As he becomes involved and presses forward, filling those roles which are open to him and seeking to invest his time and energy in that which will count most for God's kingdom, it is quite appropriate for him to "desire earnestly" the high calling of missionary or even of pioneer missionary evangelist. When multitudes of those who profess faith in Christ become this kind of actively obedient disciple, God will thrust out into the harvest field those laborers whom He has chosen.

Yet even for those who are "climbing on course" there are many ways to be deflected from God's trajectory by the Enemy. For your reference I consider briefly seventeen of these in the Appendix.

One of the best ways to tune out the Enemy's deceptions and bring in the Lord's signal with clarity is to concentrate on the principles of the Bible. We have considered many of these in the earlier chapters. We have seen God's character and God's purpose in the world. We have examined the condition of lost people, the failure of the church, and the reasons for it. We have looked at our own motives, and, in this final chapter, we have seen that God does indeed have a purpose for each of His children and that we may know that purpose. When these things come into focus, it becomes much easier to evaluate how I may best fit into God's purpose and bring together all that I am and have in a vocation and location that will most effectively promote the accomplishment of His purposes in the world. As increasing numbers of God's people become biblical disciples, committing themselves to be truly world Christians, God will be able to get through with His call to special vocations, and, using those who hear and obey, He will finish the task.

Destination

No generation of Christians has been fully obedient to Christ's Great Commission. And yet, no generation of human beings can be reached except by the Christians of that generation. For fifty-nine generations of lost people it is too late. And yet, according to the promise of God, some generation will be able to stand before the Lord and say, "It is finished. The task you have given us to do, we have accomplished."

In these latter decades of the twentieth century, we find a church fractured and weak, preoccupied with many interests other than God's chief interest. And yet, as the church prepares to give an account, we have, possibly for the first time, the potential for completing the task. The resources of people and finance, coupled with the extraordinary powers of twentieth-century technology, are ours. All that is lacking is obedience. Obedience will release the pent-up power of Almighty God to do through His church what He has longed to do throughout the centuries.

Paul tells us that the time is short (I Cor. 7:29). The time is short for any generation because each man will soon stand before his Maker. In another sense, the time is not long before another century—indeed another millennium—will have passed over a disobedient church. Again, the time is short for you and me, for we will soon stand and give an account for the investment of our lives whether poorly spent, or invested to the maximum (I Cor. 3:12ff). But Paul was speaking of eschatological time. The time is short because our Lord will soon return. What kind of people, then, ought we to be? If we love Him, we long for that time when all the wrongs will be made right and we shall be with Him forever. If we truly love Him, should we not labor to bring Him back with all speed?

Yet God tarries. Why does He delay? Peter tells us it is because He is longsuffering, not willing that any should perish, but that all should come to repentance (II Peter 3:9).

When will He return? This He has not disclosed. But He has given us a commission which, thus far, has been the great omission. And until every person has heard with understanding the way of life in Christ Jesus, and until a congregation of God's people has been established in every community, we may not give priority to any other task. It is love for the Savior, our desire to bring Him joy and to see Him satisfied on that great day which draws from us our highest and best.

Who is calling? God is. But the more crucial question is, who is listening? With the need so vast and the laborers so few, why do we not go? Someone isn't listening.

"How come?" We have heart trouble. We are so preoccupied with our own interests that there is no room for compassion for others; we are so committed to our own fulfillment that it is impossible to love God with all our lives.

"How come?" We have eye trouble. Even when we study the Bible we don't see reality from God's viewpoint.

"How come?" We have head trouble. We try to figure out all the mysteries of an infinite God and all the proper destinies of human beings. Then we play God, trying to alleviate the pain of human lostness by arrogantly setting aside the teaching of Scripture in favor of our own logical conclusions.

"How come?" We have knee trouble. We play at prayer when God has put in our reach the most powerful weapon of spiritual warfare.

"How come?" We have ear trouble. God calls, but we don't listen.

What should we then do? Should we not repent of our cold hearts, blind eyes, arrogant mind-set, prayerless lives, and deafness to His call? Let us give ourselves to prayer till He ignites us with the flame of His love and scatters us as firebrands throughout the darkness of a lost world.

Great Commission Commitment

To strengthen the purpose you find in your own spirit, it may help to make that commitment before the Lord in writing. Perhaps one of these prayers will reflect that which is in your heart:

Disciple's Pledge

By the grace of God and for his glory, I commit my entire life to obeying Christ's Great Commission. Having committed myself to this world-focused way of life, I will:

1. Pray earnestly each day for God's work of world evangelization.
2. Give sacrificially for this cause.
3. Consistently share my faith with non-Christians.
4. Seek to influence others to become global Christians.
5. Go anywhere and do anything God desires.

Signature _____ Date _____

Apostolic Pledge

It is my wholehearted intention, unless God clearly directs otherwise, to become a missionary to those currently beyond the reach of the gospel.

Signature ——————————— Date ————

Interference

1. Marriage

Second only in importance to the choice of life investment, is the choice concerning marriage. The apostle Paul makes it abundantly clear to the Christians at Corinth that for the service of Christ the single life is to be preferred. He also makes it abundantly clear that not just anyone has the capacity to live the single life in purity and contentment (I Cor. 7). The Christian who marries assumes certain obligations for his partner and any children God may give, and certain restrictions on his ministry for Jesus Christ. Paul makes it clear that neglect of family responsibilities is a great sin (I Tim. 5:8).

Many of the unreached in the world live in conditions that demand sacrifices not suitable for married people, especially married people with children. The tension is brought into even sharper focus through the constant affirmation in contemporary Christian literature that family must take precedence over work. This is held to be true even when "work" is service to God. Thus it is imperative for the disciple to discover, before marriage, whether God has gifted him with the ability to remain single for the sake of the kingdom of God. And Jesus taught that one so gifted *ought* to remain single for the kingdom's sake (Matt. 19:12). Unless a far larger number of single people make themselves available for that special relationship to the Lord and special service for Him, the difficult frontiers may never be penetrated.

On the other hand, if married people evangelize these dark corners, the commitment to spouse and children and the commitment to love God more than wife or children must be held in dynamic—if painful—tension.

Many men and women with apparently great missionary potential have been deflected through marriage to one who did not have the same burning heart. So the decision to marry and the choice of marriage partner are life-determining decisions.

2. Short-term Service

Short-term service, ranging from a few weeks to two years has been opposed as a great dissipation of the Lord's money and the time of career missionaries, but it also has been advocated as the greatest method for recruiting career missionaries. The approach is with us to stay. Therefore, to maximize the potential, we must avoid the dangers.

The first danger comes when statistics include short-term missionaries with career missionaries, giving the impression that we are growing in the task force available for frontier penetration. Actually, the statistical growth in North American Protestant missionaries during the past two decades is the result of the increasing numbers of short-termers. This must not be allowed to deflect us from the urgency of re-cruiting a vast new force of career missionaries.

A second danger would be the illusion that a per-son can test his gifts and calling for career missionary work adequately through a brief trial period. In the nature of the case, it is impossible for him to try out the real experience. The real experience includes learning the language, immersion in the culture, and a kind of commitment that rearranges all the furni-ture in one's mind. It is something like trial mar-riage—one is not trying out the reality. Yet if the short-term missionary is aware of this limitation and takes it into account, he can certainly learn many things about himself and the place of possible future service.

There are other potential problems, but if the pro-gram is well planned and carefully supervised by wise career missionaries, the short-term missionary may enter into long-term, effective service in the missionary enterprise or serve as a "world Christian" in the homeland.

3. Tent Making

There are two types of tent makers: those like Paul and those like Priscilla. Paul manufactured tents on occasion when gift income did not cover the expenses of the missionary team. Paul's calling and vocation was as a pioneer missionary evangelist. He supple-mented his income through a trade that was won-derfully mobile and flexible. On the other hand, Priscilla and her husband manufactured tents as their vocation. As true disciples, they were lay evangelists and Bible teachers, ministering in the local congregation.

Laymen who are faithful to their calling to witness as disciples and to serve with their spiritual gifts are the only hope of the church. But church history does not encourage us to believe that Priscilla-type tent makers will often penetrate the frontiers and establish the church where it has not yet been planted. For this task, tent makers like Paul are needed—that is, people who are called first of all to the apostolic missionary vocation and who, in order to accomplish this, may utilize some income-producing activity as needed.

There have not been large numbers of these "tent makers" in the annals of the missionary enterprise, though there have been some very effective ones. But there is an added need for this approach today when political and religious barriers often inhibit the entrance of professional Christian workers. The fact that 10 percent of the world's nation-states are closed to the entrance of outside missionary activity should not be inflated into the myth of "so many closed lands." There are more open doors today than ever before in church history. Furthermore, doors open as well as shut. That 10 percent includes a large proportion of the unreached peoples of the world. Thus the possibility of entrance in some role other than church-related vocation may be not only the *best* way, but the *only* way to reach these millions of lost people. To the courageous and creative, few doors are truly shut.

One caution concerning the "tent-making" phenomenon in the thinking of some young adults is that motivation must be carefully examined. Paul did not consider making tents a "cool" occupation, more socially acceptable and ego-stroking than missionary work. The offense of the Cross and the fanatical opposition he faced as a missionary were actually his glory. He exulted in this identification with Christ and did not seek to escape the opprobrium by assuming a more socially acceptable vocational label.

4. Children

Many young parents draw back from missionary commitment from fear their children will suffer. It is true that the decision to have children restricts a couple from many choices in life, no matter what the vocation of the parents. It is also true that some missionary children have had difficulty in re-entry into the American youth culture. This unfortunate experience of some, however, should not be inflated into the myth that missionary children are handicapped because of the parents' vocation. Historically and statistically, the opposite is the case. The children of missionaries have been successful spiritually, emotionally, socially, and vocationally in far higher proportions than the children of parents in other vocations, according to some studies.

I do not deny there are peculiar problems of adjustment for anyone who moves from one culture to another. However, the transcultural person also

91

has many advantages because of that breadth of experience.

On the other hand, when a missionary discovers that his situation is adversely affecting his children, my conviction is that he, like any parent in any other vocation, should probe the possibility of a radical rearrangement of either location or vocation. Yet there is the balancing truth that if one would truly be the disciple of Christ he must subordinate to that calling even his greatest and most sacred human relationships. For he who loves father or mother, wife or children more than his Lord cannot be truly Christ's disciple (Matt. 10:35–39).

If one is concerned about the possible negative effects that the environment of some distant land may have on his children, he must also honestly face the question of the environment to which his children will be exposed in his homeland. Actually, many missionaries have discovered that the environment for the missionary child is better than what would be experienced in the homeland. In any event, the bottom line has to do with the will of God. To raise children in the place of God's appointment is safer by far than to seek the ideal environment outside the will of God. The life of faith is the only answer for the raising of children wherever we may live.

5. Health, Climate

Fears for health are partly left over from the early days of missions when missionary graves outnumbered converts. Good health care is not restricted to

North America. Some parts of the world are a greater risk than others, but many of the most strategic mission fields have physical environment and health care equal to, if not superior to, that which we have in the United States.

People with disabilities and handicaps are going to the mission field in numbers which would have been unthinkable fifty years ago. If one mission board does not have opportunities for such people, others may.

There is another answer to one who makes it his ambition to preach Christ where He has never been preached—God's healing touch. I was stricken with what my doctor diagnosed as an incurable illness. God, in answer to prayer, cured the incurable. Later, I contracted tuberculosis and emphysema. But again, God rehabilitated me and sent me on my way.

If one's hestitancy concerning foreign service does not hinge on an actual health condition, but on the unpleasantness of a particular climate or the risk in a particular environment, he is thrown back to the basic question of discipleship. How much do I love my Lord, and what sacrifice am I prepared to make for Him?

6. Age

Some mission boards still restrict candidates for missionary service to those who are youthful. Most mission boards, however, have found effective roles for those of almost any age.

7. Lack of Language Aptitude

Closely associated with the question of age is the problem of real or perceived difficulty in learning another language. First of all, we should remember that there are many needy fields where English can be used. For those who actually do have a low aptitude for learning language, I would simply offer the encouragement not to give up too soon. A friend who went to Japan with me had—by test score and experience with Greek—about as low a language aptitude as could be measured. Yet through fortitude and perseverance, within a decade this missionary become fluent and adept in the Japanese language. A language considered among the most difficult was mastered, in a way few missionaries have mastered it, by one who was judged virtually incapable.

8. Lack of Evangelistic Ability

For years I asked God to give me the gift of evangelism, having in mind the American evangelist who holds large campaigns and sees hundreds or thousands responding to the public invitation. I longed to serve God at the frontiers as a church-starting evangelist, but my own faulty understanding of the gift and role of evangelism almost deflected me from pursuing the apostolic missionary career. I discovered that the way God had made and equipped my wife and me was ideal for winning Japanese to faith. We found that the American mass approach with the hard sell is not ideally suited to the Japanese. We saw that we could live among Japanese people and love them and see them turn to our Savior, establishing congregations of God's people. There are many ways in which people may be led to faith. Any one of these is effective evangelism, and the person who uses that method effectively is an evangelist equipped for the task by the Lord of the harvest.

9. Other Aptitudes

There are some who avoid even considering missionary service because they feel themselves too gifted, too well-educated, or too highly qualified to waste these superior talents on less worthy "primitive aborigines." Those who feel this way, even if the feelings are deeply buried under layers of more worthy rationalizations, need to face such pride as a destructive distortion of reality. God who became incarnate among us would not be impressed with the validity of any feeling of superiority—especially the feeling that one is too good for a vocation God puts at the head of His list.

Others, however, feel they do not have the aptitude or spiritual qualifications for so high a calling. Do I have what it takes? Many a fearful Christian has shrunk back in the company of the ten spies out of fear of failure. Let us join Joshua and Caleb in the obedience of faith! We must be freed by the realization that God is the One who equips and that He does not call without providing the resources. He delights in providing those resources for very ordinary people.

10. Training

Closely associated with the question of aptitude is the question of training and experience. Increasingly, Christian young adults are treating the scores on vocational aptitude tests as a revelation of God's will. College students and recent graduates often ask how their particular academic specialization can be used on the mission field. It is true that an astounding variety of skills may be used in some aspect of the missionary enterprise. The approach, however, is backwards. Should not the disciple inquire first of all, what is the need and what is God's call and commission to me? For this I will secure the appropriate training. The other way—to force God's program to fit the mold of various occupations that were not designed with His program of world evangelization in mind—will certainly "jam the signals."

Some students have told me they did not even enjoy the vocation for which they had trained. One said that he had not yet begun the specialization, but that his school guidance counselor had indicated this was the appropriate vocation for him because of his aptitude and the projected American market for the next decades. Missionary service was not even in the list of options, but a test and this counselor revealed the will of God!

This brings up the matter of how seriously to regard tastes, talents, and aptitudes in choosing a career. Obviously, these things should all figure in the decision. They should not, however, be allowed to weigh too heavily against the factor of current needs and opportunities, which could conceivably be more important. Under some circumstances one might actually serve God better in a crucial vocation in which he was mediocre by the world's standards than in a less strategic profession in which he might excel. Moreover, tastes, talents, and aptitudes are often more acquired than inborn and can be developed and altered through education of one kind or another

This is an acute point today because we are in the midst of a philosophy that argues for self-fulfillment, for doing your own thing, for blooming where you are planted. To be sure, God bestows special gifts that wait to be discovered and used. But there is also such a thing as bowing too low before the altar of ability. Even in the Bible, God's will for a lifetime does not always correspond to conspicuous traits.

The point is that talent is not the *ultimate* indication of what the Lord wants us to do. Nothing in Scripture tells us we must exploit some particular mental or physical capacity throughout our lifetime because we have been assigned an extraordinary measure of it (David Kucharsky "Careers with Christian Impact," *Christianity Today* [September 24, 1971], pp. 12–13).

It is strange that while young people are increasingly locking themselves into a predicted aptitude, the opposite phenomenon is taking place in the world of work where millions are making mid-career changes, ignoring the years of investment in education and experience in order to do what they perceive might prove more fulfilling.

11. The Money Issue

I am not sure that the drive for an affluent way of life is compatible with true discipleship, but the fear of financial insecurity is natural enough. To those who are deflected from missionary service for this cause, the Lord has a special word:

> "And do not set your heart on what you will eat or drink; do not worry about it. For the pagan world runs after all such things, and your Father knows that you need them. But seek his kingdom, and these things will be given to you as well.
> "Do not be afraid little flock, for your Father has been pleased to give you the kingdom. Sell your possessions and give to the poor. Provide purses for yourselves that will not wear out, a treasure in heaven that will not be exhausted, where no thief comes near and no moth destroys" (Luke 12:29–33).

There is another aspect of finance that seems to deflect increasing numbers of young adults from missionary service. The fear of doing deputation, of "begging for money," is a great barrier for many. This problem does not exist in most denominational missions, but for those who are contemplating service in a mission in which each missionary is responsible for his own support, this may be a matter of apprehension. There are several answers to this problem.

When a missionary candidate spends several years in ministry here in the United States, he develops a network of relationships that will provide a strong foundation for his future missionary work. He will not only find the financial support through this network, he will find the all-important prayer base for the more intense spiritual warfare that lies ahead.

Some missions consider deputation a crucial test

for a person's ability to relate to people, to communicate effectively, to be creative, and, above all, to trust God for his needs. They consider this the final test of one's calling. If such a mind-set is adopted, a person can move out with confidence and expect the Lord to provide through His people. He will not be asking people to give to him so much as he will be providing people the opportunity to invest part of their lives in God's cause.

12. Feelings and Honesty

If a person is still committed to doing only what he feels good about and has accepted the contemporary deception that only what is compatible with personal desire can be honest, he probably is not ready to consider any Christian vocation, let alone missions. Sometimes the most honest thing a person does is to act contrary to his feelings. He proves his integrity to his whole being—his intelligence, his commitments, his future, his relationships. Out of love for the Lord or love for others the disciple has learned to sacrifice his own desires and even his own rights. Sometimes there is the agony of Gethsemane in which one cries out for deliverance, but in the end says, "Nevertheless, not my will, but thine be done."

13. Fulfillment, Duty to Self

If fulfillment of my own potential and the discovery of that which gives me greatest satisfaction is my goal in life, I have yet to learn the meaning of discipleship, which is self-sacrifice for God's fulfillment, rather than sacrificing others or the kingdom of God for my own perceived best interest.

Although this truth is elementary, it is amazing to discover how many mature Christians, even Christian workers, make choices in life on the basis of what is likely to be personally fulfilling. Although it is quite legitimate to consider this as one piece of the puzzle, it can hardly be a major factor in the choices of a true disciple.

14. Blessing on My Ministry

Many have not seriously considered the call to missions because God has prospered them in the ministry in which they are engaged. This also is a factor which must be taken into account, but this alone is not a valid criterion. In fact, unless missions is only for those who cannot succeed in anything else, God, like any good employer, is not looking for the frustrated, the failure, the unemployable, but is looking for those who have proven themselves. In Antioch, it was the top leadership of the church that was chosen for the missionary team. Apparent blessing, or even genuine blessing, is not of itself proof that a person is in the center of God's will. Moses was preeminently blessed when he struck the rock, but he was completely out of the will of God.

15. Opposition of Family and Friends

God intends us to consider the advice of others, particularly those who are spiritually mature Christians, and He certainly expects children to honor their parents and to care for them when this is needed. However, multitudes have been deflected from missionary service by unspiritual or undiscerning, if well-meaning, family or friends. There comes a time when one must "leave the dead to bury their own dead" and move out in obedience to God's commission, trusting Him for those loved ones. When we were ready to leave for Japan no one except my semi-invalid widowed mother was in favor of the move. Every other person in our circle of friends counseled us to remain in the place of God's blessing where we were serving.

In the final analysis, I am the one who must give account for the choices I make and the investment of my life. Sometimes it is necessary to conclude, "We must obey God rather than men." Note that though Christ spoke of leaving, for His sake, brother, sister, parents, and children, He did not speak of leaving wife or husband (Matt. 19:29).

16. The Need at Home

It is often said that the need for evangelism in the homeland is so great that this should take priority. Further, we are told, until we get our own spiritual act together we should not be so arrogant and presumptuous as to export our inferior brand of Christianity to others. It is true that we must begin in "Jerusalem," our home place. It is true that we must not only win to faith but disciple believers, teaching all things that Christ commanded. It is true that a strong home base is needed to support spiritually and materially those who are sent. But these true principles must never be used as a "cop-out" to evade our responsibility for the whole world of lost people. For a person to seriously hold that we must totally "Christianize" one place before moving on to another is to condemn three-fourths of the world to hopeless ignorance of God's life-giving salvation. It is also to flatly disobey the Commander-in-Chief.

Furthermore, such a position does not make much sense in a world where there is one full-time evangelical Christian worker for every two hundred people in the United States, one for every two hundred thousand in India, and one for every two million in Algeria, for example. In fact, half the world is out of reach of present gospel witness. In such a world every local congregation is called to reach out beyond its own "Jerusalem" to surrounding "Judea," neighboring "Samaria," and, indeed, to the utmost reaches of the world.

17. The Indigenous Church Is Responsible

Many call for a temporary or even a permanent moratorium on foreign missionary personnel and finance since, it is held, the church in each nation should be responsible for the evangelization of that nation. This concept may be true for some places and in those places any foreign mission should be humbly sensitive to such an evaluation. But to extend this to a serious evaluation of the whole world of lost men and women is to betray great ignorance of the world situation.

In the first place, though there is a Christian presence in virtually every nation-state in the world, in many of them that presence is so small that it is a wonder the church even survives. To expect it to muster adequate strength to complete the task is to say with Cain, "Am I my brother's keeper?" But the even greater error in this position is ignoring the fact that half the world lives in cultural enclaves or language groups within those nation-states which have no witnessing church among them. In other words, if someone does not go in from the outside (a "foreign missionary"), there is no hope. There is no church to grow, no church to evangelize. Of course we must recognize as Americans that by "foreign missionary" we do not mean "white anglo," let alone "American." No, the missionary task of the world church is the task of the *entire* world church. It is that church, which, in some generation, will finish the war which was actually won at Calvary, vanquishing the forces of darkness and reigning with the Conqueror forever and ever.

Also from OM Literature:
Challenge of Missions
By Oswald J. Smith

Almost 2000 years have passed and the desire of Jesus that all should hear his good news is as strong as ever. In this remarkable book Oswald J. Smith maintains that the church which takes this command seriously will experience the blessing of God.

ISBN: 18845-4302-2

Also from OM Literature:
Serving as Senders
By Neal Pirolo

This key book makes the strategic point that moblizers - the senders - are as crucial to the cause of missions as frontline missionaries. It is a book just crammed with solid, exciting insights on the most hurting link in today's mission movement.

ISBN: 18801-8500-8

Heros of Faith and Courage
By Ben Alex

This remarkable series of 7 fully illustrated books is
bound to be loved by you and your children.

Hudson Taylor
The Missionary Who Won a Nation by Prayer
ISBN: 18845-4314-6

William Carey
The Shoemaker who Pioneered Modern Missions
ISBN: 18845-4315-4

Dietrich Bonhoeffer
The Pastor Who Followed Christ to the Cross
ISBN: 18845-4318-9

David Livingstone
The Missionary who "Discovered" Africa
ISBN: 18845-4321-9

Martin Luther
The German Monk who Changed the Church
ISBN: 18845-4313-8

St.Augustine
Bishop of Hippo, Father of the Church
ISBN: 18845-4319-7

Florence Nightingale
The Lady with the Lamp in Battle
ISBN: 18845-4316-2